Certainty Kills

A Primer for Approaching the Bible with
a God-honoring & Neighbor-loving
Openness

BY BRUCE PAGANO II

INK
Publishing House

Endorsements

Claims about absolute certainty have destroyed so many. Whether that certain was said to be a particular interpretation of the Bible or a particular view of God, the results are damaging. Bruce Pagano II rightly calls us to humble claims about what matters most. Certainty certainly kills.

Thomas Jay Oord, Author of *Open and Relational Theology* and many other books

Certainty Kills is a refreshing and timely challenge to how we often approach scripture and faith. In clear and compelling prose, Bruce Pagano II confronts the dangers of absolute certainty in biblical interpretation. He makes a persuasive case for why openness and humility are essential for nurturing a healthy Christian faith that honors God and loves others transformationally. *Certainty Kills* is a wise yet gentle rebuke that our faith communities desperately need in these dividing times. This primer reveals how closed systems fail us, but curiosity and committed faith foster adventure into the diverse tapestry of human experience. By promoting humility over dogmatism, Pagano calls us to recenter our faith on embodying the way of Jesus.

Dr. Thomas J. Hogan, Community Chaplain

In *Certainty Kills*, Bruce Pagano II provides a concise and compelling explanation of how the call for certainty within faith communities has negatively impacted both the external witness and internal spiritual growth of the followers of Jesus. This book is a powerful reminder that the human need to know something beyond a doubt, while sometimes necessary, can also be the root

i

cause of division and polarization. Pagano demonstrates the vast difference between rigid, dogmatic unity and the unity that grows from a desire to follow the example of Jesus.

Janyne McConnaughey, Author of *Trauma in the Pews: The Impact on Faith and Spiritual Practices*

DEDICATION

To *Technical Sergeant Richard "Ricky" Smith, USAF*
Thanks for helping me understand the importance
of being certain and when it's most helpful.

TABLE OF CONTENTS

INTRODUCTION

In 2009, before i met my wife, a significant life event caused me to lean into a newfound appreciation for contemporary Christian music (CCM). As I immersed myself in worship music, I was able to find immense healing. It was a season of life that, necessarily, restricted my musical library to a single genre. Then, in 2010, my musical world exploded when I met Sarah.

Sarah had a far more extensive music palette than I knew could exist in one person. As our friendship grew, she introduced me to many genres, most of which exist under the "indie" umbrella. At the same time that our friendship was growing, I had a friend who was diagnosed with a rare form of leukemia. I was in the military then, and they allowed me to spend a lot of time with him and his wife in the hospital. We lived in Cheyenne, Wyoming, and they admitted him to the Aurora, Colorado, hospital. I spent a few times each week driving the three-hour roundtrip to spend time with them. During those drives, I consumed so many new bands and songs. It was both a comforting and necessary distraction.

One of the bands that Sarah introduced me to was *Death Cab for Cutie*. If you've never heard of them, put this book down and Spotify them. Death Cab's whole discography is fantastic, but one song remains a psalm of lament and remembrance for that time of my life. The song is, *What Sarah Said*. As if sharing a name with my now wife wasn't enough, the song's lyrics perfectly reflect the profoundness and difficulty of that experience.

Initially, my friend handled the treatment well. At one point, it seemed like the doctors had eliminated the cancer, and he just had to wait for a bone marrow transplant. While most days it was clear that the treatment made him physically weak, he was often in good spirits, and it showed in his typical joking and laughing. Then, almost out of nowhere, he started getting worse. Initially, the doctors didn't know what was going on with him. After numerous tests, they discovered that he had a severe infection but were unable to pinpoint where it was in his body.

During these frequent trips to the hospital, I eventually realized that although I enjoyed Sarah's friendship, I wanted to be more than friends. I was new to the dating scene again, so I had no idea how to approach this new desire. Regardless, life circumstances weren't right for our relationship to transition, so we remained friends. That's an important detail because our friendship was an immense source of comfort as I watched my friend get sicker.

I can't remember if, eventually, the doctors decided that it was necessary to put my friend in a medically induced coma or if he just slipped into one. I think it was the doctors, and I remember them hoping that the coma would give him the best chance of treating the infection because the cancer treatment had destroyed his bone marrow, leaving him with no immune system.

While he was in his coma, I still went and visited my friend. Often, I just sat there and watched his wife sit by his bedside. She talked to him, often through tears, held his hand, begged for him not to die, and sometimes laughed as she reminded him of a funny story; I like to think he knew she was there and heard her. As I sat there and watched her and him, the song, *What Sarah Said*, echoed in my head. The song is sung from the perspective of a person standing in a hospital waiting room, anticipating bad news about a loved one's medical condition.

As the song brings you into the waiting room, with all the smells and sounds, it swells to this stanza:

'Cause there's no comfort in the waiting room.
Just nervous paces, bracing for bad news.
And then the nurse comes round,
And everyone lifts their heads.
But I'm thinking of what Sarah said…

And what did Sarah say? She said, "Love is watching someone die." The song ends by asking, "So who's gonna watch you die?"

That line screamed in my head as I sat in my friend's ICU room and watched his wife watch him die. Up to that point, and maybe not since, I had never had the privilege to see such raw love unfold –

a person, wracked with sobs, helplessly watching their other leaving this world. My friend passed away after just over a week of being in a coma. His family allowed me the honor of being there with them and him. They even asked me to pray with them. And, contrary to some ridiculous military policy, they insisted that I be allowed to escort him to his home state to be laid to rest.

That was 13 years ago. I think of my friend often. I think of the privilege of knowing him and the honor of being with him and his family at the end. I think of sitting there and watching him and his wife as Death Cab's question echoes. There was a moment during that week when I understood the song and the depth of love it took for my friend's wife to sit with and watch him die. As that realization came over me, I questioned who would watch me die. The only answer I could come up with was my friend, Sarah.

I was absolutely certain I wanted it to be her.

Certainty

Adjective, 'sər-tᵊn-tē: something that is fixed or settled

While the title of this book may cause you to think I'm opposed to the idea of certainty, I promise you, I'm not. There are a lot of benefits to being certain. Certainty can bring confidence, allowing a person to make decisions and act without hesitation.

In some situations, certainty can help contribute to a stable and predictable environment, fostering a sense of security and order. Certainty can lead us to make firm commitments, whether in relationships, faith, or personal goals. Certainty provides an essential sense of clarity and direction and can help to establish a firm foundation for our beliefs, values, and decision-making processes.

I do not intend to suggest that certainty is unhelpful or is something we should avoid; as I mentioned, there are positive aspects of being certain. Instead, this book will focus on the danger associated with how some Christians believe they are absolutely certain about the accuracy of their individual or religious institution's interpretation of scripture.

In and of itself, handling scriptural interpretation with absolute certainty might not seem to be a problem. However, it is problematic because it informs and forms belief systems and doctrines that negatively impact how adherents treat and interact with each other and others, especially those outside their established belief system.

This book is not intended to be an exhaustive discussion of the dangers of developing, and adhering to, a belief system grounded in the absolute certainty of your interpretation of scriptural texts. Instead, it is intended to be a primer, which is to say it's an introduction to how absolute certainty can threaten a healthy and welcoming expression of your faith.

As you read through the book, each chapter will include three parts: how certainty kills that attribute that is necessary for a healthy faith expression; why that attribute is necessary for a healthy faith expression; and how you might invite that attribute into our faith journey.

For clarity, a healthy faith expression in the context of this book honors and reveals a loving God, manifest in the teaching and example of Christ, by recognizing, acknowledging, and interacting with all others as divine image bearers. To that end, this book is intended to promote the importance of rejecting the mindset that your interpretation of scripture is the only one.

The title is probably more provocative than it needs to be. Still, the title is necessary for getting the point across about how potentially dangerous absolute certainty of our scriptural interpretations can be.

When I say dangerous, I'm not being hyperbolic. There is a growing pool of data that connects spiritual harm and religious abuse to the way in which religious leaders interpret and teach specific passages of scripture. [1] The degree of absolute certainty with which religious leaders deliver their teaching can easily result in harm and abuse that impacts their adherents, and encourage "Christians" to promote, support, justify, or participate in dehumanizing behaviors, or even worse, violence, against those "outside" their belief system. Some of those "others" might be those they oppose in the abortion debate, people who vote Democrat, and, historically, many who are part of the Black, Indigenous, and People of Color (BIPOC) community.

This absolute certainty around biblical interpretation has been particularly egregious regarding Christian's interactions with those in the Queer community. Attempts to "correct" those in the Queer community with fundamental theology have involved a spectrum of "tools," including teaching self-hate, forced conversion therapy, and even complete rejection and exile from the religious community. All of these things continue to

---

[1] Start Here: Koch, D. and Edstrom, L. (2022), Development of the Spiritual Harm and Abuse Scale. Journal for the Scientific Study of Religion, 61: 476-506. https://doi.org/ 10.1111/jssr.12792

contribute to and result in the increasing suicide risk in that community.[2]

This book intends to encourage an openness regarding scriptural interpretation that results in an understanding that contributes to a healthy faith expression and creates welcoming, safe, and inclusive communities for all Image-bearers.

All Types of Certainty

Certainty, as a concept, is not inherently good or bad. Depending on the context and how it is being approached and applied, it can carry positive and/or negative consequences with it. With that in mind, it's best to understand the different types of certainty before moving forward.

Because this is a primer on how absolute certainty of your scriptural interpretation impacts the essential attributes of a healthy faith expression, this will not be a philosophical deep dive into the different types of certainty. Instead, I'll briefly introduce the different kinds of certainty and then focus the rest of the book on how absolute certainty prevents an openness that honors God and others.

The Internet Encyclopedia of Philosophy (IEP)[3] identifies three types of certainty: objective, epistemic, and psychological (subjective). In addition

---

[2] According to a 2022 report of the Trevor Project, "...LGBTQ young adults ages 18–24 found that parents' religious beliefs about homosexuality were associated with double the risk of attempting suicide in the past year."
[3] IEP, https://iep.utm.edu (a peer-reviewed academic resource)

to the IEP, I also used the Stanford Encyclopedia of Philosophy (SEP)[4] and other publications to formulate the following descriptions. Information about the fourth type of certainty, absolute, comes from Religions Wiki[5] and the references identified therein. So that I don't have to make reference notes every other sentence, I'll say upfront that the following definitions and descriptions are my attempt at paraphrasing and summarizing, as simply as I can, what I read from those sources. Let's start with objective certainty.

Objective certainty is an assurance grounded in verifiable evidence, logical reasoning, and empirical observations. Often, it relies on facts and information that are rigorously examined and subjected to experimental scrutiny. As much as possible, it looks to minimize subjective interpretation and bias. Achieving objective certainty involves scientific methodologies, critical thinking, and a commitment to rigorous investigation. An example of objective certainty is that water boils at 100 degrees Celsius at normal atmospheric pressure based on repeatable trials and scientific agreement.

While similar to objective certainty, *epistemic certainty* is a broader concept related to the confidence a person has in the knowledge and beliefs they hold based on the available evidence and the reliability of their sources. It involves a more

[4] SEP, https://plato.stanford.edu/entries/certainty/
[5] RW, https://religions.wiki/index.php/Absolute_certainty

comprehensive evaluation of knowledge, considering not only verifiably observable evidence but also critical thinking, logical reasoning, and adherence to accepted standards of inquiry. Epistemic certainty recognizes the temporary nature of knowledge and remains open to questioning and revision. Examples of epistemic certainty are any scientific theories supported by extensive empirical evidence, peer-reviewed research, and adherence to the scientific method.

Psychological or subjective certainty is a personal confidence or belief in a particular idea or perspective rooted in feelings, emotions, and experiences. We develop subjective certainty by psychological factors such as cognitive biases, emotional states, and past experiences. It may not always align with externally verifiable or objective evidence. An example might be a person's deep, passionate conviction that a superstition brings them good luck despite a lack of observable evidence. Subjective certainty also includes a person's belief associated with their religion.

A close cousin to subjective certainty is *absolute certainty*. This is closer to the type of certainty with which most religious people approach their beliefs. This type of certainty is a belief accepted beyond any level of doubt, reasonable or otherwise. It's typically connected to a type of argument that cannot be proven or disproven by any evidence because it is based solely on what the person deems logical. The belief in God is a common example of this type of certainty. For the person who believes in God, all the evidence for God existing is based purely on what the believer deems as logical beyond any doubt. Specifically, for the believer in creationism, it is not logical that creation sprung out of nothing, so logically there must be a creator. For the person who holds this belief, this argument cannot be explicitly proved right or wrong.

Regarding how we interpret scripture, the difference between absolute and subjective certainty is in the practical application of our formed theology. For our purposes, a person's unwillingness to extend consideration and engage in open dialogue about alternative interpretations or views indicates absolute certainty. Attached to that premise is the assertion that two people cannot have fellowship or be relationally connected unless they believe exactly the same way.

Alternatively, subjective certainty suggests that although a person is confident in their belief system and how they arrived at a particular interpretation of scripture, they express a willingness to extend consideration and engage in open dialogue regarding differing beliefs and interpretations be-cause it does not threaten their belief system. Because of that, they are willing to build and maintain healthy and mutually edifying relationships, regardless of differing belief systems.

Certainty Kills

With those foundational assumptions, the remainder of the book will explore how absolute certainty harms a healthy faith expression and interpersonal relationships and the preference for subjective certainty within our personal and communal religious belief system.

The Opposite of Certain

When you look at the definition of *certain* you'll see positive words like *dependable, reliable, known or proved to be true, indisputable.* If you Google, "the opposite of certainty" a couple of the main results are *uncertainty* and *doubt.* Again, there are some important benefits to being certain, but at face value the positive words can cause you to believe that uncertainty and doubt are negative attributes to have. It's not true. Doubt can be a useful tool.

Mark 9 tells a story about a man seeking Jesus to heal his son from a spirit. When Jesus asks him if he believes He can heal him, the man replies, "I believe; help my unbelief!" The implication is that the man trusted that Jesus could heal; likely, he had seen or heard about it happening to someone else. But, even with that trust, there was still doubt that the same could be true for him.

In that moment, the man struggled between what he knew to be true and what he doubted was possible for his son. His doubt was just as honest and essential as his belief because he came to Jesus with an openness and vulnerability that revealed his more profound need: to know God cared for him and his son.

I want to propose an alternative to uncertain as the opposite of certain. What if *openness* is the opposite of absolute certainty? What if we were willing to be open to the possibility that we got an interpretation of scripture wrong or even that our belief is too restrictive to reflect the goodness of God? What would change if we were open to the possibility that other people's views of God are more comforting and inclusive than our belief system allows for, without it threatening our relationship with Jesus? How would our faith and relationships grow? Regarding how we understand scripture, the opposite of certainty should be openness.

If we desire to approach scriptural interpretation and understanding with openness, it is helpful to remember the difference between Jesus and the rabbis in his day. There was a reason that Jesus would often start his teaching by saying, "You have heard it said... but I say..." This is a corrective and declarative statement. Jesus was correcting the misinterpretations and misunderstandings of well-established Jewish doctrine. Religious leaders and teachers were certain about their interpretations of their scriptural text, to the degree that they created a vast system of doctrines around their understanding of the text. These were doctrines that undergirded the entire Jewish culture. And yet, Jesus shows up and asks His disciples to be open to Him correcting these deeply held beliefs, that, again, they were certain were indisputably true.

How can we be so pompous as to believe that we understand and interpret scripture better than the people who established doctrine based on the text that Jesus grew up reading? And yet, Jesus still sought to clarify their understanding. Are we so fixed and settled in our interpretations of scripture that we are no longer open to Jesus saying, "You have heard it said… but I say to you"? Our call is to be disciples, which means we are to be learners. Openness to new understandings of the biblical text reveals our commitment to being a disciple.

The type of certainty we should approach our religious beliefs with is subjective certainty. Subjective certainty allows you to be open to scriptural interpretations that lead to a healthier expression of faith and empower you to love others fully. It provides a steadfast commitment to your God, while allowing openness toward others because their faith or beliefs don't threaten yours.

Alternatively, absolute certainty will always cause you to put your belief system before relationships with others. Because of this, many Christians who approach their understanding of the bible, and ultimately their belief system, with absolute certainty do so with an unspoken or unrealized fear that their belief system cannot stand against what they deem as secular ideas.

Certainty

Unfortunately, this certainty forces them to double down on their interpretation and defend its believability and seriousness, lest it all comes tumbling down. Sadly, many Christian belief systems program the idea of openness out of them for fear of being tossed about as waves, having our ears tickled, and being led astray by the devil himself.[6]

When it comes to understanding scripture, the older I get, the more open I am to the idea that I might be wrong. That's not to say I don't feel confident about related things. I'm sure of my belief in who Jesus is and what He taught about caring for and loving others. When we extend our certainty beyond our faith in Christ and how He desires to make us fully human and a divine reflection of the God-image, we begin our path toward becoming unteachable and departing from discipleship.

In his book, *Faith After Doubt*, Brian McLaren asks an important question that deals with this idea of faith and belief. He asks:

> What if the deeper question is not whether you are a Christian, Buddhist, or atheist, but rather, *what kind of Christian, Buddhist, or atheist are you?* Are you a believer who puts your distinct beliefs first, or are you a person of faith who puts love first? Are you a believer whose beliefs put you in competition and conflict with people of differing

---

[6] Ephesians 4:14, 2 Timothy 4:3, Mark 13:22

beliefs, or are you a person of faith whose faith moves you toward the other with love?

Let's start building from that place: faith that moves you toward the other with love.

Certainty

Certainty Kills

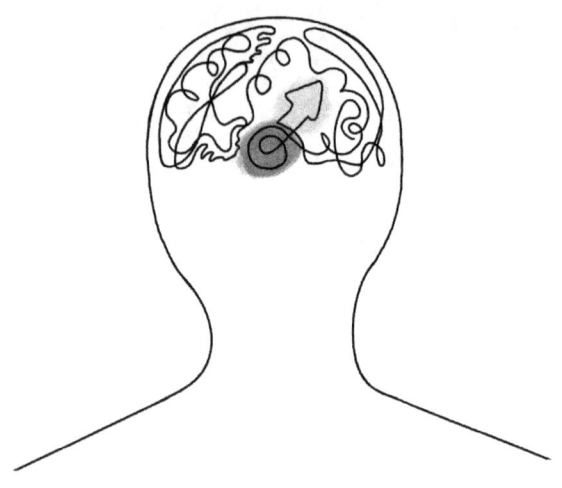

Conscience

Noun, 'känSHəns: … an internal sense or voice of right and wrong that guides behavior

How Certainty Kills Conscience

Absolute certainty in one's interpretation of biblical scripture can twist a person's sense of morality, profoundly affecting their conscience. Becoming entrenched in their belief system can foster an "ends justifies the means" mentality. This mentality can lead to the searing of the person's conscience, allowing them to justify actions they deem "biblical." When this happens, the ultimate goal becomes an adherence to their scriptural interpretation to the degree that it overshadows the moral and ethical means by which they apply that understanding.

In this scenario, the conscience, which should act as a moral compass, becomes dulled, causing the person to justify any action contrary to the core Christian values of love, kindness, and justice in service to their interpretation. This erosion of the conscience is particularly dangerous because it can lead, and has led, to justifying harmful behaviors based on religious conviction. An unwillingness to examine those convictions can make us justify belief structures that exclude others as part of a faithful and "biblical" way of life.

Certainty Kills

Not thinking deeply about how our actions affect others can make us lose touch with the actual purpose of following Jesus. Ultimately, the danger of interpreting the bible with absolute certainty is that it can dull a person's moral sensitivity. This dulling makes it easier to defend actions or beliefs without considering the consequences and how they impact real people.

The Importance of Conscience

Conscience is critical to the healthy functioning of relationships, acting as a mechanism for evaluating the quality of our behavior while considering another's perspective with an intention toward understanding. The central role of conscience is to align our actions with our core moral or religious beliefs, ensuring that our actions reflect who we are at the core of our character. For Christians, our belief in and desire to demonstrate Christlike love and compassion should shape and form our conscience.

It's crucial, therefore, to approach biblical interpretation with humility and openness. Recognizing that our understanding is limited and subject to fallibility can help us maintain a healthy and active conscience. This approach allows us to be guided not just by our interpretations but also by the Holy Spirit, who leads us into all truth and helps us to discern God's will more accurately.

Conscience

Inviting Conscience

Cultivating a healthy conscience in light of biblical interpretation involves healthy questioning and evaluating our understandings. It requires a commitment to seeking God's truth beyond our preconceived notions and interpretations. A humble and open approach to interpreting biblical scripture acknowledges our limitation to fully understand.[7]

Conscience invites us to self-reflect. This self-reflection ensures our beliefs and actions embody the love, forgiveness, and service to others that Jesus taught. Our conscience should also drive us toward communal accountability and diverse interaction with the intent to know ourselves and others more clearly. Engaging with a community of believers, embracing diverse perspectives, and being open to correction can all contribute to a more well-rounded and healthy conscience.

A well-formed conscience, not seared by absolute certainty, is continually refined by a humble, seeking heart that desires to align more closely with God's love for all. In the next chapter, we'll see how a healthy conscience paves the way for a genuine, curious spirit toward God's Word and our world.

---

[7] 1 Corinthians 13:12

Certainty Kills

Curiosity

Noun, kyu̇r-ē-'ä-s(ə-)tē: a desire to learn, ask questions, and engage with others

How Certainty Kills Curiosity

Curiosity is vital to our faith, yet absolute certainty in one's interpretation of biblical scripture can severely stifle it. When we hold unwaveringly to our interpretations of scripture, we tend to close ourselves off from exploring the perspectives or others. This certainty leads us to view different interpretations of, and experiences with, the bible as irrelevant, unimportant, or worse, as a threat. Such an attitude diminishes our capacity for growth and learning and hinders our ability to engage meaningfully with the diverse body of Christ.

Lack of curiosity can also lessen our empathy, reducing our desire to engage with and understand others. Empathy is an essential human trait and a hallmark of Christianity. One of the primary ways that allow us to grow more empathetic is through curiosity and connection to others. Because we often fear what we don't know, the absence of curiosity that builds our empathy can cause us to become defensive and live in fear of others and how they understand and interpret biblical scripture.

Refusing to be curious limits our spiritual journey to a road defined only by preconceptions and interpretations. This limitation can lead to a faith which is stagnant, and one lacking in the richness and depth that comes from exploring the vast and varied landscape of biblical understanding present in the global Christian community.

The Importance of Curiosity

Curiosity leads to deeper understanding, resulting in a more profound faith experience. It encourages us to ask questions, seek new insights, and engage with others meaningfully. Curiosity drives us to explore beyond the confines of our current and comfortable space. This exploration allows us to consider the possibility that God can speak to us in new and unexpected ways, specifically through the diverse interpretations and experiences of others.

Embracing curiosity in our approach to scripture allows us to discover the multifaceted nature of the bible and what it means to be a Christian. It helps us appreciate the bible's richness, which has spoken to countless individuals across different cultures and historical periods. Curiosity leads us to a more empathetic and compassionate engagement with others as we seek to understand their perspectives and experiences rather than dismissing them outright.

Curiosity

Inviting Curiosity

Fostering curiosity within our faith journey requires an intentional effort to step beyond our comfort zones and engage with ideas and interpretations that challenge our own. This can be done through diverse community involvement, where different viewpoints are expressed and valued. It involves a commitment to lifelong learning (discipleship) and an openness to the guidance of the Holy Spirit, who often leads us to truths that defy our expectations and challenge our preconceptions. The openness to being guided reveals a more genuine expression of trusting the Holy Spirit to lead you into all truth.[8]

Reading widely, engaging in discussions, and being willing to ask questions—even those that might seem unsettling—can all stimulate curiosity. By doing so, we follow in the footsteps of the Bereans, who the writer of Acts commends for examining the Scriptures daily to see if what Paul said was true.[9]

As we conclude this chapter on curiosity, we pave the way for the next chapter, "Context," highlighting the importance of understanding the bible's historical, cultural, and linguistic background. Curiosity drives us to dig deeper into these areas, enriching our understanding and applying God's Word.

---

[8] John 16:13
[9] Acts 17:11

Context

Noun, 'kän-ˌtekst: the surrounding elements of a discourse that provide meaning

How Certainty Kills Context

Absolute certainty in one's interpretation of biblical scripture can be a significant barrier to under-standing how to approach and apply biblical teaching. This certainty often leads us to ignore critical discourse and information that provides the necessary context for understanding scripture. Contextual understanding includes knowledge of historical, cultural, and linguistic backgrounds of biblical texts, and is essential for a compassionate and just application of its teachings. Failing to understand these critical context areas can cause us to read and apply biblical texts through a modern and, for many of us, a western cultural lens, missing the more profound elements and opting for more literal application.

Without an appreciation for context, we risk interpreting scripture in ways disconnected from its original intent. This disconnection can lead to applications of scripture that are at odds with the overarching message of love and justice central to the Christian faith. Extracting verses and applying them to situations without considering their historical or cultural setting and original intent can result in interpretations that harm rather than heal and exclude rather than include.

The Importance of Context

Understanding the historical and cultural context of biblical text is crucial for comprehensively and accurately interpreting their messages and modern usefulness. The bible, composed over centuries in a shifting and forming culture and in languages far removed from our contemporary context, presents a rich tapestry of history and spirituality. An appreciation of the nuances and complexities of the times the writers penned the biblical text opens us to a deeper understanding of the writer's message, intentions for the reader, and God's desires for humanity.

Contextualization of the text is crucial for interpreting the text more inclusively and compassionately. This contextualization involves recognizing the diversity within the biblical narrative and seeing how God has interacted with humanity throughout biblically recorded history. It helps us discern how to apply these timeless truths to our present circumstances in a way that better reflects Jesus and His teachings.

For instance, understanding the cultural and historical context of first-century Israel is essential when considering the story of the rich young ruler, as recorded in Mark 10:17-27. Context reveals that wealth was often accumulated through social inequality and exploitation.[10] Thus, the narrative isn't just a simple condemnation of wealth but a profound critique of a socio-economic system that allowed some to accumulate wealth at the expense of others. It challenges us to consider how wealth gained at the expense of others contradicts the compassionate and just life that a follower of Christ is called to lead.

A context-informed approach to scripture enriches our understanding and enables us to apply its principles in our daily faith practices. It encourages us to approach scripture with humility and a readiness to learn rather than with a rigid certainty that leaves no room for further insight or more profound understanding.

Inviting Context

To form a deeper contextual understanding of scripture, we must be committed to studying the historical and cultural backgrounds of the bible. This commitment involves engaging with biblical scholarship, which can shed light on the ancient Near Eastern and first-century Mediterranean worlds. It means being open to insights from archaeology, history, and linguistics, which can bring the world of

---

[10] Kakwata, Frederick. (2015). An inquiry into socio-historical factors contributing to poverty within the Early Church in Palestine. *In die Skriflig* , *49*(1), 1-10. https://dx.doi.org/10.4102/IDS.v49i1.1993

the bible to life in ways that enrich our under-standing and expand our spiritual journey.

Furthermore, in addition to reading scripture on our own, forming an appreciation for context means reading it within a community of believers. This community should include our contemporaries and the great cloud of witnesses throughout church history who have wrestled with these texts and sought to apply them in their contexts.

As we wrap up this chapter on context, we set the stage for the next chapter, "Critical Thinking." Understanding the context of scripture sharpens our ability to think critically about its application today, helping us to apply its teachings in ways that are both faithful to its original intent and relevant to our contemporary world.

Context

Certainty Kills

Critical Thinking

Noun, ˈkridək(ə)l ˈTHiNGkiNG: objective analysis and evaluation of an issue before forming a judgment

How Certainty Kills Critical Thinking

Absolute certainty in one's interpretation of biblical scripture can significantly impair critical thinking, especially regarding spiritual discernment and application. In our attempts to interpret and understand biblical text, the rejection of critical thinking can inadvertently lead to blind alignment and rigid adherence to a specific teaching or teacher, regardless of its coherence and alignment with the compassionate teachings of Jesus.

Additionally, a closed mindset limits personal growth and can foster an unloving attitude toward others, potentially creating an environment where those with different beliefs are demonized rather than understood. The danger lies in the possibility of following teachings that skew or misrepresent Jesus's message simply because they resonate with our preconceived notions or interpretations in a way that forwards our personal agenda or those of our institutions. Such a lack of critical engagement can lead to a faith practice that, while appearing devout, may stray far from the compassionate, justice-oriented teachings of Jesus.

Certainty Kills

When we dismiss critical thinking, we risk pigeonholing ourselves into a belief system based solely on inherited teachings and personal preferences. This unquestioning acceptance may overlook inconsistencies or interpretations that don't align with the core principles of love and compassion, which are central to Christianity. In doing so, we can potentially distort biblical truth into a rigid dogma that excludes thoughtful examination.

Without critical thinking, believers may inadvertently adopt unloving attitudes toward those whose perspectives differ, leading to their demonization and creating an environment where we see differences as threats rather than opportunities for growth and connection.

The Importance of Critical Thinking

Critical thinking in our faith journey is not about skepticism for its own sake, but about seeking truth with a discerning heart and mind. It involves the evaluation of interpretations, teachings, and religious practices against the central message of the life and teachings of Jesus. This process is vital for ensuring that our faith remains grounded in the true essence of Christianity – a life based on love, acceptance, and forgiveness.

Engaging critically with our beliefs and teachings enables us to avoid being swayed by every new doctrine or charismatic leader that comes our way. It helps us to distinguish between what is culturally or denominationally specific and what is central to a Christian faith. Critical thinking necessarily safeguards against distortion and manipulation, keeping our faith practical.

Inviting Critical Thinking

Developing critical thinking in our spiritual lives involves a few essential practices. One practice involves regular and intentional engagement with the bible, that includes studying its background, contextual interpretation, and thoughtful application.

It might also involve being a part of a community that welcomes questions and is willing to discuss different viewpoints respectfully. Such a community encourages growth and learning as members provoke one another to love and good deeds.[11]

Critical thinking in interpreting scripture should involve prayer, contemplation, and reflection, focused on seeking the guidance of the Holy Spirit as a counselor, and a community of faithful believers as co-sojourners, in an attempt to apply Jesus's teachings in our lives wisely.

Much like understanding the context of scripture enhances our ability to think critically about its application today, critical thinking helps discern the

---

[11] Hebrews 10:24

truth in our faith journey and leads us to understand and appreciate how cultural nuances play a crucial role in living out our faith in diverse ways, while not allowing for an inflation of our own culture as superior to another.

Critical Thinking

Certainty Kills

Culture

Noun: ˈkəlCHər: the customs, arts, social institutions, and achievements of a particular group

How Certainty Kills Culture

Absolute certainty in one's interpretation of biblical scripture can harm how we view and interact with different cultures. This form of certainty often leads to an overvaluation of one's cultural expressions and practices as being more aligned with biblical principles. This perspective can foster a dismissive or destructive attitude toward other cultures, their values, and their ways of expressing faith. When we read the bible believing that our interpretation is inarguably correct, we can unintentionally fall into a dangerous trap of assuming that our culture—how we live, celebrate, and see the world—is the ultimate standard.

This assumption can make us less tolerant and even fearful of differences. We quickly begin to see our cultural practices as the standard because we tie them so tightly to our interpretation of scripture, thereby making everything else seem less important or even wrong. Then, we effortlessly conflate Christian culture with our national culture, causing us to double down on the "rightness" of how we believe culture should look. This doubling down can close our eyes to the richness of diversity and stifle dialogue, breeding conflict between us and those we deem "outsiders." The evidence for this is the rhetoric within many churches to "change the culture" and the active participation by many Christians in a perceived "culture war," which comes with a willingness to dismiss, degrade, or destroy other cultures.

When we interpret scripture solely through our culture's lens, we risk losing the richness and diversity that different cultural perspectives can and do bring to our understanding of the Christian faith. We also risk alienating those whose cultural expressions of faith differ from ours, potentially causing division within the body of Christ. It is a stark reminder that when faith becomes entwined with a sense of cultural superiority, it risks becoming an instrument of division rather than unity.

The Importance of Culture

Acknowledging and valuing cultural diversity is crucial in our faith journey. Culture influences how we interpret and live out Jesus's teachings. Recognizing this helps us appreciate that no single cultural interpretation is fully comprehensive or definitive for being a Christian or even just a human being. Each culture brings unique insights and expressions that can enrich our collective understanding of the Kingdom of Heaven as we welcome it to Earth.

Embracing cultural diversity within Christianity helps us see the Gospel's universal nature – as a message for all people from every nation, tribe, and tongue. This understanding fosters a diverse unity as we celebrate how God's truth is understood and lived out in different cultural contexts.

Inviting Culture

To form a healthy appreciation for cultural diversity, we must first acknowledge our own cultural biases and be open to learning from others. This involves listening to and learning from people with different cultural backgrounds to understand their perspectives and experiences.

It also means being aware that we read and study the bible through our own cultural lenses. We must be willing to question whether our cultural context influences our interpretations and be open to the possibility that other cultures might offer valuable insights that challenge or enrich our understanding.

Forming an appreciation for culture requires humility and a willingness to accept that all people are image bearers and valuable, regardless of whether they are Christian. This acceptance helps us to understand that, within Christianity, the kingdom of God transcends any single earthly culture. To that end, it's about embracing that our unity in Christ is not based on uniformity in cultural expressions but on our shared faith in Jesus.

Understanding and embracing cultural diversity enriches our faith, and part of embracing other cultures is developing an appreciation for the multiple aspects of the creativity that is inherent in various cultures. Creativity plays a vital role in expressing and living out our faith in a constantly changing world.

Culture

Creativity

Noun, ˌkrēāˈtivədē: the use of imagination or original ideas to produce art or other works

How Certainty Kills Creativity

When absolute certainty governs our interpretation of biblical scripture, it can severely constrain our appreciation for creative expression in our pursuit of God. This rigidity can lead us to view new ideas and perspectives as threats, stifling our ability to innovate and apply Jesus's teachings in culturally relevant ways. Our spiritual life demands creativity to engage with an ever-changing world and to express the Gospel's timeless truths in a manner that resonates across diverse cultures.

Though we strive to follow biblical principles, we should hold our interpretations humbly, acknowledging that fellow Christians may derive different understandings about the same passages. Insisting that our view is the only faithful one can hinder our ability to be creative in finding new ways to fulfill Christ's commandment to love our neighbors.[12] This is especially true when engaging with non-Christians whose belief systems may differ markedly from our own.

---

[12] Mark 12:31

Certainty Kills

By humbly embracing creativity in how we communicate the teachings of Jesus, we avoid the arrogance accompanying rigid dogmatism. Instead, we open doors to sincere dialogue and foster an environment where our humanness can flourish. This mindset allows us to creatively connect with, and serve, others in the most Christlike manner possible, following Jesus's example of inclusive love and service rather than erecting walls based on perceived theological threats.

Christlikeness means embodying love, grace, and humility in every interaction while holding our beliefs gently, inviting others to creatively express their faith in ways that best enhance their relationship with God. Through this openness and creativity, we can genuinely fulfill Christ's call to love God, our neighbors, and each other, expanding the reach of the Gospel by demonstrating its relevance and power in today's world.

The Importance of Creativity

Creativity is a divine gift, allowing us to explore different practices for expressing our faith. It enables us to connect with God and others in authentic, immersive, and culturally sensitive ways. Creative expressions of faith can take many forms, from the arts to problem-solving, storytelling, and how we organize and do church. Embracing openness in our interpretation of scripture allows us to apply biblical teaching creatively. This can help us move beyond literal and traditional understandings into more profound meanings and applications. This openness enables us to engage with the bible as an active text that speaks to the diverse situations and challenges of our time.

Christians should actively embrace creativity as we seek to apply our understanding of biblical teachings to modern life. The bible can guide the development of a moral value system, yet how we live out Christlike values can and should vary across cultures and eras. Jesus demonstrated this creative application of scripture through His parables, contextualizing spiritual truths within compelling stories that resonated with His audience. He also chastised the Pharisees for rigidly following the letter of the law while violating its spirit - principles of justice, mercy, and faithfulness.[13]

Similarly, the early church showed creativity by adapting their historic Jewish customs to fit their new understanding of Jesus as the Messiah and His new covenant. The apostles developed innovative ways of structuring church leadership and worship gatherings, enabling the Gospel to transcend cultural barriers.[14] Today, we should seek to continue this tradition of creative adaptation. We must avoid dogmatic, narrow, and formulaic interpretations and instead develop innovative ways to apply

---

[13] Matthew 23:23
[14] Acts 2:42-47, Acts 15, 1 Corinthians 14

meaningful scriptural principles to our modern world.

Through prayerful study, communal devotion, and considering context and cultural nuances, we can honor others by applying Christ's teachings in a way that does not compromise our value system and embodies the wisdom of scripture in vibrant and life-giving ways for all cultures and people.

Inviting Creativity

Fostering creativity in our spiritual practice requires an openness to the Holy Spirit's leading and a willingness to step outside our comfort zones. It involves engaging with the arts, culture, and the world, seeking inspiration from diverse areas of human creativity.

It also means being part of a faith community that values and encourages creative expression. Such communities are places where somebody can explore new ideas and where diverse expressions of worship and service are welcomed and nurtured.

Practically, we can cultivate creativity by experimenting with different forms of prayer and bible study, incorporating the arts into our worship and devotional life and being open to new ways of doing ministry and community life.

By engaging with various forms of art, culture, and other forms of creativity, we can begin to enhance life within our community. Whether it is

Creativity

trying different prayer styles or incorporating art in our worship, we should remain open to the Holy Spirit's guidance and perhaps take the opportunity to explore previously unfamiliar territory. Valuing and nurturing creative expression within the body of Christ is vital as we seek to enrich our community.

Certainty Kills

Community

Noun, kə'myoōnədē: shared attitudes, interests, and goals that create fellowship with others

How Certainty Kills Community

Absolute certainty in one's interpretation of biblical scripture can inadvertently undermine the value of diversity within a religious community. This certainty promotes unity based on strict adherence to specific theological rules and dogmas rather than fostering unity centered on Jesus Christ, creating what author Mark D. Baker calls a bounded church.[15] Such an approach often leads to a homogeneous community in thought and practice, discouraging differing viewpoints and interpretations that could otherwise enrich the collective faith experience.

When Christians become rigidly set in their theological convictions, insisting theirs is the only faithful interpretation, it fractures our unity and hinders the development of a healthy Christian community. This rigidity can stifle the spirit of community, as it places boundaries around who is "in" and who is "out" based on specific interpretations of scripture rather than on the shared belief in Jesus. It limits the capacity of the community

---

[15] Baker, Mark, D. (2021). Centered-Set Church: Discipleship and Community Without Judgment. (Intervarsity Press Academic: Downers Grove, IL)

to learn from, and be enriched by, the diverse ways in which different members experience and understand their faith.

Paul's appeal to the Corinthians, "that all of you agree with one another so that there may be no divisions among you and that you may be perfectly united in mind and thought"[16] is a call to unity based not on dogmatic certainty but on a common call to follow Jesus and embody Christlike love. Insisting on conformity to our interpretive paradigms stunts diversity within the body of Christ and signifies a lack of trust in the discernment of fellow believers.

Healthy Christian fellowship does not emerge by enforcing uniformity, but through open dialogue in an atmosphere of grace guided by a desire to love one another. [17] We must allow room for different applications of biblical principles to cultural contexts. Despite varied conclusions on secondary issues, our shared devotion to living out Christ's teachings unites us. It is with humble certainty that we can build up the Church, embracing the rich tapestry of diverse thought and experience that each member brings to our collective faith journey.

The Importance of Community

Community is at the heart of the Christian faith. The New Testament church exemplifies a community of

---

[16] 1 Corinthians 1:10
[17] John 13:34

believers who, despite their differences, were united in their devotion to Jesus Christ. This idea of fellowship underscores the importance of diversity within the church, acknowledging that each individual contributes unique insights and experiences that enhance the collective understanding and practice of the Christian faith.

No Christian should expect to comprehend scripture perfectly, especially in isolation. We need fellowship with other believers to gain balanced, nuanced interpretations that show up in our Christlike behavior. In community, we combine varied experiences and gifts to strengthen mutual discernment.

Unity in Christ does not equate to uniformity in thought or practice. Instead, it encourages a fellowship that welcomes diverse perspectives and unifies members around their shared commitment to follow Jesus and His teachings. Love, mutual respect, and a shared desire to grow in faith all mark such a community. It is in this spirit that the early church, through communal discernment guided by the Holy Spirit, resolved the dispute over Gentile inclusion.[18] Their decision to embrace Gentiles into the church demonstrates the transformative power of community in action.

When we humbly engage with fellow Christians to understand and apply scripture, we access wisdom that eludes us when alone. Accountability to

---

[18] Acts 15:1-35

a Christian community ensures that we live out Christlike values while remaining open to how these values might take shape across different cultures and eras. Only through a devotion to a Christian community can we gain the discernment necessary for how we live out Jesus's teachings in a way that allows us to live in peace with others[19] and garner the goodwill of all the people.[20]

Inviting Community

We must first recognize and acknowledge our biases and limitations in understanding scripture to foster a community that values diversity and unity in Christ. We must be willing to listen to and learn from others, especially those who may see things differently. Creating space for open and respectful dialogue is crucial. Creating this space can happen through small groups, communal dialogue, and other settings where members feel safe to ask questions and express their views.

Additionally, we should seek to center community life around practices that unite rather than divide – such as worship, gathering together, and sharing in the Lord's table. These practices remind us of our shared faith in Jesus and our collective call to imitate Him.[21]

---

[19] Romans 12:18
[20] Acts 2:47
[21] Ephesians 5:1-2

Community

As we conclude this chapter on community, we prepare to delve into the next chapter, "Connection." Just as a healthy community fosters unity in diversity, so does the concept of connection, which encourages us to reach beyond our immediate circles to engage with and learn from the broader world.

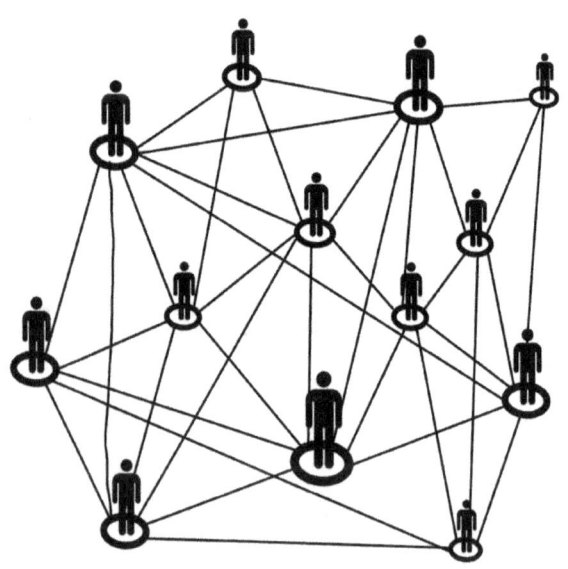

Connection

Noun, kə'nekSH(ə)n: the relationship between individuals, things, or ideas

How Certainty Kills Connection

Being absolutely certain about our interpretation of scripture can lead to isolation and hinder our engagement with the world. This fear-driven withdrawal limits our exposure to the diversity of God's work and narrows the Gospel's impact on both our own faith journey and the faith journeys of others.

This self-righteous isolation can foster a false sense of superiority, blocking the development of meaningful relationships and reducing our empathy. Although our commitment to our specific understanding of scripture may be rooted in faithfulness or tradition and stem from the noble intention of adhering to a "biblical worldview," it creates a rigid dogmatism. This dogmatism can distract us from the valuable perspectives of our historic Christian predecessors and those of our contemporaries who presently seek to challenge us into a more profound faith.

Our reluctance to step outside our comfort zones means we miss out on the rich experiences and insights others have to offer. We fail to find common ground for mutual understanding without openness and the willingness to connect. Such behavior stands in stark contrast to the example of Jesus. He connected with people across societal boundaries and challenged religious leaders to move beyond rigid absolutes to embrace humility and genuine relationships in a way that elevates others and humbly lowers themselves.

The Importance of Connection

The essence of the Gospel is relational and calls for connections within and beyond our religious circles. These connections enrich our faith by acknowledging and recognizing every individual as an Image bearer of God. These relationships, whether formed inside or outside our faith community, lay the groundwork for growth in Christ. They challenge and refine our faith by exposing us to diverse perspectives, strengthening our beliefs, and maturing us emotionally, relationally, and spiritually.

Connections are fundamental for personal development and the means through which love, the primary element of the Gospel, spreads. The teachings of Jesus compel us to build bridges and enact God's love broadly, not limiting ourselves to our immediate faith communities. We see this exemplified in the early church, where the disciples and later the early church fathers, encouraged and fostered connections within the community that garnered the goodwill of all the people.[22]

Our commitment to inclusivity should echo the approach of Jesus, who connected with individuals from all backgrounds, including those outside the religious mainstream, regardless of their social status, ethnicity, or gender. This inclusive nature fosters a sense of belonging and offers others a glimpse of Jesus's beauty. Moreover, through these genuine connections, we can apply His teachings more effectively in our current cultural context, addressing real needs and transcending ideological barriers.

Ultimately, our willingness to connect with others indicates our trust in the Holy Spirit's function and enables us to live out a more genuine and visible faith. These connections within and beyond the church walls are crucial to inviting and experiencing heaven on earth.

Inviting Connection

We must cultivate a spirit of openness and curiosity to form meaningful connections beyond our immediate religious circles. This means actively seeking relationships with people who think, believe, and live differently than we do. It involves listening to

---

[22] Acts 2:47; Justin Martyr, Tertullian, Origen argue extensively that Christians are honorable, valuable, and devoted citizens.

their stories, desiring to understand their perspectives, and working to find common ground.

We also need to foster a secure foundation in our faith that allows us to engage with different views without fear. This can happen through regular spiritual disciplines such as prayer and study with our Christian community.

Additionally, forming connections involves intentional actions - participating in local community events, volunteering in diverse settings, and being present to meet and interact with various people without making them our evangelism projects.

As we close this chapter on connection, we pave the way for the next chapter, "Compassion." Just as forming connections with a wide range of people is crucial, so is the development of compassion, which allows us to empathize with and serve those whom we encounter in our interactions.

Connection

Compassion

Noun, kəm'paSH(ə)n: a sympathetic concern for others' suffering or misfortune

How Certainty Kills Compassion

Absolute certainty in one's interpretation of biblical scripture can profoundly impact our ability to express compassion. This kind of certainty often leads to a disconnection from people and cultures different from our own, and hinders our ability to see them as fellow image-bearers deserving of compassion and kindness. Our insistence that our understanding is the only correct one makes it easy to overlook the needs, struggles, and humanity of others, particularly those outside our immediate faith community.

The danger of this self-righteous claim to our perfect interpretation is that we may become judgmental, seeing our perspectives and faith practices as the only righteous way. This leads to a rigid adherence to moral paradigms, with little room for empathy for those we consider "outsiders." Then, we begin to see alternative understandings and interpretations as threats fostering an "us-versus-them" mentality focused on proving our righteousness and superiority rather than humbly serving as Christ did.

Certainty Kills

Christ himself associated with those the religious elite considered unclean, emphasizing love over law. Even when He engaged the law, Jesus chose compassion over condemnation. Recognizing that no one has a complete or perfect understanding of anything allows us to hold our interpretations humbly. Absolute certainty creates an empty Gospel, betraying the core values of love, kindness, and compassion for all.

The Importance of Compassion

Compassion is central to the Christian faith; it reflects God's heart and the life of Jesus. Deep compassion for the marginalized, the outcast, and those we might otherwise deem "sinful" marked Christ's ministry. Our call as Christians is to emulate this compassion in our interactions with others, viewing them through love and grace rather than judgment and exclusion.

Expressing compassion leads to a more authentic representation of Christ's love. It breaks down barriers, builds bridges, and opens doors for human flourishing. Compassion also enriches our spiritual lives, aligning our hearts more closely with God's heart and deepening our understanding of grace.

Inviting Compassion

Forming a compassionate heart requires an intentional effort to see beyond our preconceptions and engage empathetically with the world around us. It involves actively seeking to understand the experiences and perspectives of others, particularly those who suffer or are marginalized.

Practicing compassion can start with small, everyday acts of kindness and empathy. It also means advocating for justice and standing with those who are vulnerable or oppressed.

Compassion also humbles and cautions us against developing overly rigid interpretations. Connecting Jesus's teachings to human needs requires examining varied perspectives and a willingness to adapt when our paradigms prove inadequate. Our study of scripture should expand our capacity for empathy. Then, we interpret and live out biblical principles in ways that lift the brokenhearted, not wound them further.

As we conclude this chapter on compassion, we transition to the final chapter, "Christlikeness." Compassion is a crucial attribute of Christlikeness, and as we grow in compassion, we move closer to the fullness of the character and mission of Jesus Christ.

Certainty Kills

Christlikeness

Adjective, ˈkraɪstˌlaɪk: embodying the spirit of Jesus Christ

How Certainty Kills Christlikeness

Absolute certainty in one's interpretation of biblical scripture can, ironically, lead us away from Christlikeness. This form of certainty breeds self-righteousness and spiritual pride, making us unteachable, closed to the Holy Spirit's trans-formative work, and prone to condemnation of others rather than compassionate connection. This attitude starkly contrasts Jesus's humility and openness to all, regardless of their background.

Self-righteousness stunts our spiritual growth and impairs our ability to connect with others in a genuine way. We become preoccupied with defending our beliefs, which causes us to lose sight of embodying the love, compassion, and humility of Jesus. This mindset departs from true discipleship, which involves continual learning and growth, to become more like Christ in all areas of our life.

Absolute certainty limits fellowship to those who mirror our beliefs and lifestyle, neglecting Jesus's practice of engaging diverse people with radical inclusion. This approach blocks collaboration with those who think differently, distorting our ability to see the worth in everyone as Jesus did.

Certainty Kills

Ultimately, when our certainty hinders meaningful self-reflection and openness to the perspectives of others, we cease progressing toward emulating Christ's sacrificial love. Embracing openness and wisdom, rather than just certainty, allows us to apply biblical principles in increasingly Christlike ways, honoring the diverse experiences and needs of those we encounter.

The Importance of Christlikeness

Because Christlikeness is the ultimate goal of the Christian journey, we should seek to embody and reflect the fruit of the Spirit[23] seen in Jesus. It's about living out the values and principles Jesus taught, impacting the world through our actions, words, and attitudes. This path requires us to stay open to the Holy Spirit's guidance and the wisdom and insights of our faith community.

As Christians, our calling is to consistently reflect the character of Jesus and apply His teachings in all interactions with everyone. This commitment prevents us from compartmentalizing our faith and being selective about extending grace. Christlike humility and compassion in our dealings, whether with fellow believers or non-Christians, honors God and strengthens our gospel witness. Embodying Jesus's radical kindness without condemnation,

---

[23] Galatians 5:22-23

especially toward those outside our faith, demonstrates that we are His.

Our interactions, even with potential adversaries, are opportunities to model Christ's humble spirit of love, which can diffuse tension and pave the way for restorative work. True Christlikeness cannot be faked; it requires a deep connection to others and a continual willingness to meet others where they are. When our character mirrors Jesus, we become more invitation-minded and draw others to the hope and light He offers. Embracing this journey means cultivating unity amid diversity, enabling all to use their gifts, and living a life marked by Christ's inclusive and selfless example.

Inviting Christlikeness

Developing Christlikeness begins with acknowledging our need for God's grace and a willingness to be shaped by Jesus's teachings, the transformative power of the Holy Spirit, and a community of faithful believers. It involves a daily commitment to seek to understand and apply Jesus's teachings to our lives.

Practicing spiritual disciplines such as prayer, meditation, fasting, acts of service and justice, and studying scripture are essential in developing Christlikeness. Engaging in a community is also crucial. Being part of a body of believers allows us to practice the critical aspects of Christlikeness of love, forgiveness, service, and humility so that we might carry them into all other personal interactions.

Serving others selflessly and lovingly, especially those marginalized or in need, is a powerful way to grow in Christlikeness. It reflects Jesus's ministry, where He consistently reached out to those overlooked or undervalued by society.

As we conclude this final chapter and the book, we circle back to the essence of our faith – a call to be like Christ in every aspect of our lives. In doing so, we counter the dangers of absolute certainty. This will allow us to approach the bible with a God-honoring and neighbor-loving openness that enables God to do transformative work on our hearts and minds so that we might love more fully and inclusively.

Continued Readings

As mentioned in the first chapter, this book is a primer or a small introductory book on a specific topic. As we've walked through the different ways that absolute certainty of our interpretation of biblical scripture negatively impacts a healthy expression of our faith, specifically as it relates to interacting with others as divine image bearers, my hope for this book is twofold.

I hope that readers will become motivated to seek a better understanding of what it means to approach the bible with a God-honoring and neighbor-loving openness. I also hope you end this book with a desire to invite and grow the attributes of conscience, curiosity, context, critical thinking, culture, creativity, community, connection, compassion, and Christlikeness in a way that draws you closer to others as you draw closer to God.

To help you on that journey, I've compiled a reading list that will take you further into releasing certainty, embracing doubt, and encountering a more profound faith experience.

Faith After Doubt: Why Your Beliefs Stopped Working and What to Do About It, Brian D. McLaren

Sixty-five million adults in the U.S. have dropped out of active church attendance and about 2.7 million more are leaving every year. *Faith After Doubt* is for the millions of people around the world who feel that their faith is falling apart.

Using his own story and the stories of a diverse group of struggling believers, Brian D. McLaren, a former pastor and now an author, speaker, and activist, shows how old assumptions are being challenged in nearly every area of human life, not just theology and spirituality. He proposes a four-stage model of faith development in which questions and doubt are not the enemy of faith, but rather a portal to a more mature and fruitful kind of faith.

The four stages - Simplicity, Complexity, Perplexity, and Harmony - offer a path forward that can help sincere and thoughtful people leave behind unnecessary baggage and intensify their commitment to what matters most. *(Publisher's description)*

The Sin of Certainty: Why God Desires Our Trust More Than Our "Correct" Beliefs, Peter Enns

With compelling and often humorous stories from his own life, bible scholar Peter Enns offers a fresh look at how Christian life truly works, answering questions that cannot be addressed by the idealized traditional doctrine of "once for all delivered to the saints".

Enns offers a model of vibrant faith that views skepticism not as a loss of belief but as an opportunity to deepen religious conviction with courage and confidence. This is not just an intellectual conviction, he contends, but a more profound kind of knowing that only true faith can provide.

Combining Enns' reflections of his own spiritual journey with an examination of scripture, *The Sin of Certainty* models an acceptance of mystery and paradox that all believers can follow and why God prefers this path, because it is the only way by which we can become mature disciples who truly trust God. It gives Christians who have known only the demand for certainty permission to view faith on their own flawed, uncertain, yet heartfelt terms. **(*Publisher's description*)**

Benefit of the Doubt: Breaking the Idol of Certainty, Gregory A. Boyd

In *Benefit of the Doubt*, influential theologian, pastor, and bestselling author Gregory Boyd invites readers to embrace a faith that doesn't strive for certainty, but rather for commitment in the midst of uncertainty. Boyd rejects the idea that a person's faith is as strong as it is certain. In fact, he makes the case that doubt can enhance faith and that seeking certainty is harming many in today's church.

Readers who wrestle with their faith will welcome Boyd's message that experiencing a life-transforming relationship with Christ is possible, even with unresolved questions about the bible, theology, and ethics. Boyd shares stories of his own painful journey, and stories of those to whom he has ministered, with a poignant honesty that will resonate with readers of all ages. *(Publisher's description)*

For those who've accepted their doubt, have deconstructed, or are currently rethinking their faith and are looking for a new way forward in developing their vision of God, consider this book.

God After Deconstruction, Thomas Jay Oord & Tripp Fuller

Deconstruction is hard! Bad views of God and harm-ful experiences lead many of us to deconstruct. But we're right to run from the nonsense we've been taught and from those who hurt us. *God After Deconstruction* will not be welcomed by tradition-alists. It's not a book for people who want the status quo or who think conventional theology works. It isn't for people who just want to tweak a bit what they've been taught.

[Oord] and [Fuller] offer an open and relational vision of God. This vision makes sense; it fits our experience; it's livable. The open and relational view aligns with our deep intuitions about love and freedom. *God After Deconstruction* is for those deconstructing and those wanting help after deconstruction. It's for people in the fire and those with scars. *God After Deconstruction* is an adventure for lovers in tumultuous times!
(Publisher's description)

www.ingramcontent.com/pod-product-compliance
Lightning Source LLC
Chambersburg PA
CBHW060254150626
46553CB00019BA/2291